TO: AnitA
6 Lion

May God Bless you,
And may you see His
Glory, As you read
this!

(signature) 3/20/04

In Time Publishing & Media Group
75 East Wacker Drive, 10th Floor
Chicago, Illinois 60601.

Visit our website at www.intimepublishing.com

Printed in the United Sates of America
Cover Design by Marc Moran
Layout of Cover by Leslie Anderson for In Time Publishing

The Library of Congress Cataloging-in-Publication Data

Monica Young-Freeman
Loosed As I Went, I Was Healed
Monica Young-Freeman

ISBN 0-9746384-4-7

LOOSED

As I went, I was Healed

by Monica Young-Freeman

The Miracle

As I Went, I Was Healed: Pain and Suffering As Pathways to Discovering Meaning and Purpose in Life

TABLE OF CONTENTS

Loosed

ACKNOWLEDGMENTS

Gratitude:

To God Almighty, who has shown me *1 Corinthians 2:9*

> *But as it is written, what eye has not seen and ear has not heard and has not entered into the heart of men, all that God has prepared (made and keeps ready) for those who love Him, who hold Him in affectionate reverence, promptly obeying Him and gratefully recognizing the benefits He has bestowed.*

God will always be the reason for my existence. All Hail King Jesus!

To my husband, Alan Freeman:

I met him in April 1996, after the storm was over. He knew nothing about me when we met, and he has never discouraged me from writing this book. Many days he came home from work, and there would be no meal prepared, nor did he receive any pampering. Instead, he would say nothing and would go into the other room to let me finish what I was doing. I also thank him for letting me be who I am, even when he did not understand my ways and decisions. He knew how important this book was to me, and I believe he knew God had allowed me to sur-

vive so I could write it. After marrying me, he told me, "The greatest impact you have had on my life
is that you are living a God-like life, and you are being a vessel of God to draw me closer to the Lord!"

I felt so honored. I thought about the Scripture **Proverbs 11: 30 (AMP)**

> *The fruit of the (uncompromisingly) righteous is a tree of life, and he who is wise captures human lives (for God as fisher of men, he gathers and receives them for eternity).*
> *I thank you and I love you, the love of my life.*

To my pastor, Bishop Arthur M. Brazier:
I cannot say enough about him. He is truly one with a Shepherd's heart. Without God ministering through Bishop Brazier to us, I know I would not have been able to stand on the word of God through my valley experiences. Often a church takes on the mantle of the Shepherd of that flock, and I have been blessed abundantly to be able to establish Godly friends within my church because of bishop's example. I once heard my pastor preach a sermon saying that when God comes back for him, he wants to hear God say, **Matthew 25:21 (AMP),**

> *Well done, you upright (honorable, admirable) and faithful servant! You have been faithful and*

trustworthy over a little; I will put you in charge of much. Enter into and share the joy, which your master enjoys.

It would take a book in itself to express my gratitude to Bishop Brazier. I describe him as a man of integrity and character, sold out to the Lord! **To Dr. Sammie Dortch,** I thank you for listening to me and for providing me with critical feedback. **To my family,** I thank you for being there for me, loving me back to wholeness. My sister Deborah Edwards, who, as long as God is willing, has always and will always be there for me. I love you so very much. My Aunt Charlotta Young-Moore, the ROCK of the family who God has blessed to outlive her many illnesses and to "keep on moving."

I thank you for enlightening me about our family history and the many positive things you told me about my early childhood. I thank you for being a mother to me while I was growing up and for always having an ear to listen and a suggestion to offer. You are loved! My cousins and nephews have been the same as my siblings throughout my life. I thank you for your many acts of kindness. Just to name a few, you were there during those many days and nights I was in the hospital. You were there when I needed a place to live; when I needed to bathe; when I needed to be taken to the doctor for follow-up care. My young cousin Quinton, three years old, would come into the bedroom to check on me and say in such an innocent and sincere way, "Whatcha saying, Monica?" My jaw was wired, and it was hard to understand my words. Thank you, Quinton. To my aunt on my father's side, Judge Blanche and my half-sister and half-brother who all came to the hospital and prayed. Blanche let me use her laptop PC to type words to express myself to others. I say, "Thank you."

To the Intercessors (Prayer Warriors) of Apostolic Church of God:

Thank you for your many countless prayers and deeds. I won't try to name everyone for I am certain I will unintentionally forget someone. But I must mention a few of the faithful who supported me. My girlfriend Gail Ratliff, after the doctor had removed all of the various devices from my body enabling me to walk to the washroom, was there to attend to me. My body and hands were still stiff and sore, after lying in bed for twelve days, and I could not wipe myself. She did it for me. What a humbling experience for me! More than anything, this was a great outward sign of love on her part.

Marcie Richards, a friend in the Lord and one I had not been in touch with for many years, came to the hospital and was my private duty nurse. She stayed over night with me until I was discharged. She would bathe me, comb my hair and pray with me every night. She would then leave and go to her day job. NO CHARGE. She would not accept money. Talk about

God having rams in the bush. I am eternally grateful to you, Marcie.

There was Evangelist Carla Carter. What a warrior! She demonstrated that she is a love-filled individual who put her life at risk for me. When a gun was pulled on me, she came to my rescue, along with Deacon Cortez Trotter, to try to apprehend the person with the gun. She was also the one who brought inspirational music for me to listen to while in the hospital.

I can never forget Leola Stuttley who turned her prayer room in her home into a recuperating room for me when I left the hospital. Allowing a hospital bed and other medical equipment to be placed in the room, it became my spiritual sanctuary. She put a bell beside my bed so when I needed to get up, she would come to assist. She refused the money my family offered her. She said, "This is what God wants me to do."

To beloved Edna Thompson, the warrior who allowed me to stay at her apartment so I would be closer to hospital therapy, four days a week.

There was my Godmother, Zarlene McKinley, who went with me through some of my most dangerous praying experiences. I remember telling her during my recuperation when my face still displayed some paralyses, "No man is ever going to look at me again." Her reply was, "Do you think that God is not going to finish the work he has begun?

It is for His glory." Yes, God finished it!

To Curtis Barnes, Minister Jerry Taylor and so many others, who never let me lose focus of the vision to write this book, thank you. You were sent by God to make sure I fulfilled God's purpose for my life.

To the many others who gave cards, monetary gifts, hugs, words of encouragement and continued prayers, I say, "Thank you and great are your rewards in heaven. For what is done in secret, God will reward you openly." All of you will always be part of my miracle! To Gwynda Jones and Parthina Ramsey, who thought enough of me to name their daughters after me. What a great honor!

To my friend Timothy Houston, I confided in him before my miracle, and he still remains very dear to both my husband and me. Thank you for your unconditional love.

To Jean Branon, the editor who gifts made this a better book.

To Janine Boynes, the typist whose diligently corrected several versions of this manuscript.

Monica Young-Freeman

INTRODUCTION

Seeds are planted early in life.
God works in mysterious ways -- ways
often unbeknown to the one upon whom
He had poured out His Spirit.

Often people wonder about their purpose in life. They may ask, "Why was I born?" "Why am I living?" "Do I have a reason to be here?" Unfortunately, some never gain any real knowledge concerning their value in the great scheme of life. I'm blessed to be able to say that I have learned and understand that I have a God-given reason for living. (We all have.) The trials I have lived through have been for spiritual growth and for the gaining of more profound and deeper God-given insights. The experiences I have lived and suffered through were all lessons to be learned. These lessons have taught me *to trust God in all things.* They have also taught me to feel empathy for and to have understanding of the pain of others. This pain and suffering can be anything related to the physical or emotional or mental health of an individual. Too often the reactions of shame, guilt and anger cause us to deny and repress our suffering and cause us to blame ourselves for the pain inflicted upon us by others. Often, our self-esteem is severely damaged in the process until we become aware of the choices we make and their

15

consequences. These patterns begin in our childhood and continue through adulthood, attracting people with abusive tendencies into our lives. This attraction can act as a powerful magnet until we become aware of why we made certain choices. Early experiences with abuse can also result in our becoming the abuser.

Frequently, this unbroken cycle of abuse and suffering occurs in silence. Obviously, there are exceptions. Everyone who is abused does not internalize their experiences and misdirect the anger into becoming self-abusers or abusers of others. Those exceptions, however, seem to be rare.

I am not a social worker, psychologist or counselor. But the evidence of healing in my life, lets me know that I can provide some insights for those who are training for these professions. I can be of assistance to those who recognize the cycle of abuse in themselves or someone they know. It is in the encountering of situations of personal pain and suffering that God has allowed me to be sensitive to the pain in others. Thereby, He has taught me the value of sharing the unspeakable.

Although the story that follows is told through the voice of one woman I call Jada, the names have been changed to protect the privacy of the individuals.

The vision to write this book appeared seven years ago when I began to question the value of what I had to share. Eventually, I found that I could no longer ignore what God had birthed in me or the fact that others waited to be set free. What

I know is that many survive and rise to be overcomers, and not always solely through therapy. Spiritual healing occurs because of others who have shared experiences and have written or spoken words to encourage, offer hope and unconditional LOVE. Often, we are silent and keep the family secrets within the walls of the home because of our fear of shame and rejection. The longing to cry out to be heard, to be set free and still be loved can create such crippling, internal conflict, resulting in the perpetuation of the cycle of abuse.

Within me there is a still small voice that I call the Holy Spirit. It is because of the presence of the Holy Spirit and voices used by and through God that I am compelled to write this book. I have known God as a protector who gives us the courage to speak the unspeakable. Throughout this book, God, Jesus and the Holy Spirit will be mentioned. There is so much to be shared relative to the significance of the spiritual. Consequently, another book will follow this one. A book in which I will specifically address the power of spiritual and religious experiences in helping us to live our God-intended purpose.

I had intellectual concerns about writing this book. The questions kept playing in my head: Should I appease others by not speaking so much of God? Will the book be seen as written by a religious fanatic? But God kept placing in my spirit, "Write the truth and let it be known; it is for My glory!" The importance of glorifying God was also repeatedly reinforced in me when I heard the testimony of others as they spoke of their experiences with healing and reconciliation. It was, is and shall forever more be God who brings us through.

It is my hope that as you read this book you will feel the experiences. You will feel them, not to judge but, so you may learn and share with others that might be suffering from emotional and/or physical abuse. If you see yourself anywhere in this book, know that you are not alone and you can be healed!

Chapter One

NECESSARY LOSSES

Everything moves in slow motion. In spite of my prayers to God to deliver me from death. I have no assurance that they will be answered. It is strange to be faced with the fact that the legal system can't protect me. I run. I hide, but I am not really out of the sight of the one I fear will snuff out my life.

I lose count of the number of times I creep quietly to the door of my apartment, thinking I hear his footsteps. Just to find, when I look through the peephole, the only sound is the pounding of my heart. I return to sitting in total darkness and silence, waiting, listening and watching. I know he is coming. What I don't know is when and where! There is no one to comfort me. I am alone by choice because I feel this is one way to protect innocent individuals from being harmed. I am reminded that even though no other person waits, listens, and watches with me, God is present in this dark night of the soul. I have copies of Scripture from the Bible and have taped them to the lampshade and walls around my bed.

I wait, listen and watch in the room that is beginning to feel as if it is my coffin.

I think of the number of times I have managed to escape my husband's crazed behavior. I also vividly recall an incident when I thought I was alone, and, at least momentarily, safe. The one determined to harm me steps out of the tub from behind the shower curtain. Oh, God! I am fright-ened, just remembering. There is no escaping this man. He tracks me down in another city, cancels my bankcard, spies on those brave enough to sit with me and pray for my safety. Not even the sanctuary of my church is safe. He vio-lates the Police Order of Protection as he sits in watch in the balcony. Upon leaving the church, he pulls a gun from his coat and tries to force me to leave with him. He runs when others come to my rescue --- safe this time. But what about the next time? Strange when this person, bent on destroying me, leaves and attends his own church as if nothing has happened.

How do I respond to others when asked why I stay in this marriage? I hear their long list of, 'I would have . . . .' I know these comments come from people who have not been stalked, who have not walked in my shoes. 'Why not relocate?' is a frequent question. I tried but he found me. My problem is complicated by being married to a man who is obsessed with possessing and controlling me; who does not value his own life. A lethal combination!

'A coward dies a thousand deaths and a brave person dies but once."

In spite of the silence, waiting, listening and watching, the day when I can't escape comes. The red sparks and the bullets coming from the gun pointed directly at me, find their mark. They leave me with no where to run, no where to hide. Soon the fear and pain is quieted by a loss of consciousness. It is as if someone placed a blanket over my mind..

Where does one begin when sharing a deeply-buried, painful life experience with another? Is it in the here and now, or from the beginning of the pain? The pain is often so deep, it does not allow even sleep to provide a place of temporary escape. There is no set place from which a life story must unfold. It depends upon the person. Some people must start from where they are, others from where they have been, and, yet others, where they hope to be. Whatever makes the

Loosed

*telling easiest marks the place from where I have
discovered I must begin.*

Jada, age 47, rapidly reviews her life in her mind's eye,
and, after sharing the chilling words above, declares that indeed
her story has two or three beginnings. She has had three oppor-
tunities to be born. One was her womb birth, then a moving
spiritual salvation as an adult, and the third rebirth was her miracle of God's deliverance from the hands of death. As she
remembers the time of her third birth, Jada quietly moves into
sharing the story of her first and actual birth experience.

*At the age of twelve and a half, my mother gave
birth to my sister. I was born three and a half years
later. During her pregnancy with me, my mother
lived in a home for unwed mothers. I was named
after a nurse in the hospital where I was born. I
remained in the home attached to the hospital
until I was three years old. At that time my mother
brought me home.*

Jada stops for a moment as she protects herself from
being pulled back into the insecurity of a time long past. She
begins speaking again;

*I was four when I lived over a tavern with my
mother, sister, grandfather and his girlfriend.*

22

Monica Young-Freeman

Some nights when I awakened to go to the bathroom, I found my grandfather with a black eye and there was blood in the sink. I remember my mother having an older, blonde female friend.
They were always together.

The impressions that remain in the mind of a child can seem peculiar when they are recalled from an adult viewpoint. But, yet, they meant something then and still do. It is just a question of discovering the meaning of these impressions.

Jada smiles as she recalls some things she still finds amusing,

In the midst of the pain, there were also some funny things. Like the time the dog chewed my mother's false teeth because she had eaten barbecue. She removed the teeth without cleaning them. There was also the time when the dog knocked over the fish bowl and ate the goldfish. I also remember the fun we had when I was taken to the bowling alley.

The joy of those moments is short-lived. Jada continues,

At age five, we moved to a better neighborhood. The unpleasantness came when I had a lengthy stay in Cook County Hospital for a third degree burn from the radiator in the bathroom.

23

This resulted in my having a skin graft. I would cry whenever my mother left.

This early experience seemed to foretell of later experiences of feeling frightened and alone without the protection of a mother.

We made another move that only included my mother, my sister and me. It was during this time that I first noticed that my mother stayed out over some of the weekends. I remember hunger, not only for love but also for food. One weekend, when my mother didn't come home, my sister baked a cherry pie and macaroni from boxes for us. There was no other food in the house.

Though Jada's elementary school years started in public schools, at age eight she transferred to a Catholic school. Although her family, was struggling financially, she thinks her mother chose a Catholic school because the children wore uniforms. It would save her money for school clothes. Jada recalls a situation when her teacher wanted to help,

The teacher pinned a note to my uniform asking if it was okay for her to give me some shoes and shirts. I remember walking home many days dragging my feet because the soles were detached from my shoes.

Once again, she thinks of fun days with her sister,

It had snowed and on the walk home from school, we would lie on our backs in the snow and use our bodies to make impressions of angels.

Once, we were coming home from school and had just gotten off the bus. My sister had to 'use it.' She told me, as we walked along and were two blocks away from the bus stop, she wanted me to push her. It would then look as if she fell and got wet from the snow. When my sister got up from the ground, there was this big yellow spot. I laughed all the way home.

Even with all the negativity in her childhood reflections, Jada continues to think of incidents that were good. She makes comparisons with other children as she says,

In fact, our life was similar to the hardships other children go through. It is often hard to remember the good things until you think about some of the details in your past.

During this time Jada's mother had another female friend who would, from time-to-time, come to visit and stay over. This friend had a cottage in Michigan, and the family would periodically visit her in Michigan. Jada laughs as she says,

Loosed

What I remember most about this situation is that this friend was much older than my mother. She had huge breasts that hung to her waist. When my sister and I would see her bra in the laundry, we would laugh.

An example of Jada's starvation for love and attention is illustrated in the following incident when her sister began to show interest in boys.

My mother's only requirement was that my sister did not have company while my mother was away from home. My sister, however, let her boyfriend come up to the inside door. I was jealous because my sister's attention, no longer on me, was being given to boys. I threatened to tell my mother. One day my sister's boyfriend asked for some water, and she told me to get it. I went to the bathroom and got the water from the toilet. As the boy was drinking the water he was saying how good and cold it was. I said, 'It should be, it came from the toilet.' To escape my sister, I locked myself in the bathroom until my mother came home.

Jada's grandmother died when Jada was a toddler. She had very little contact with her father's family as a child. Jada had an aunt (her mother's sister) and cousins. Jada and her sister spent a great deal of time with their aunt and cousins. When the family got together during holidays, Jada recalls the fun she had because she loved dancing with one of her distant cousins while the family watched.

Those visits did not always result in pleasant memories. Two episodes caused Jada to be concerned about her mother.

Like so many weekends at home, my mother did not return to us one weekend when we were staying at my aunt's house. This time something unusual happened. My aunt told me my mother got locked up for drunk driving.

The other time I worried was when one of my mother's friends was in a terrible automobile accident after leaving a tavern. We feared our mother was with her. Later, we found out that she was not. She was just 'missing in action.'

I liked this friend the best, because she was always nice to my mother, sister and to me. She lived in a nice building and always displayed feminine traits.

The next move the family made was when Jada was nine years old, and this, she recalls, was when her life really began to change for the worse.

My mother met a woman who wanted to help

27

raise us. We moved into her one bedroom apartment, and my sister and I slept on blankets on the living room floor. My mother and the woman, we were told to call her 'Aunt,' slept in the bedroom. My mother was drinking and her behavior was moody and embarrassing. To add to the embarrassment, my mother's friend dressed in men's clothing. When I asked why this was, I was told that it was because of the type of work she did.

My mother allowed the friend to raise me while she, seemingly, was more partial to caring for my sister. Although 'Aunt' took me to expensive stores and paid to have my hair done every week, she abused me verbally. When I cried and asked my mother why she allowed her friend to treat me in this manner but continued to protect my sister, I received no answer.

'Aunt' instilled fear in me and warned me to stay away from boys. 'All they want is to get into your pants,' she informed me. She gave me examples of what boys would do - - put their penises in pop bottles to 'get off.'

I became even more fearful of 'Aunt' when I discovered she treated Mother as if she were a disobedient child. She punished her by beating her with a belt until my mother's nose bled. She basically controlled whatever my mother did. Mother's drinking increased during this period, and she would punish me for the least thing. As 'Aunt' became more controlling, I felt more hopeless.

I never remember being told verbally that I or my sister were loved by my mother or 'Aunt.' My mother's friend showed her feelings by buying me things. Once, when my chores were not finished, 'Aunt,' who worked nights, woke me up and put my sister out of the room. She taped my mouth with duck tape, twisted ironing and extension cords together and whipped me. This, to me, was just more proof that my mother did not love me. She allowed her friend to mistreat me.

In sharing these deeply buried memories, they appear to be crystal clear in Jada's mind. This is so because they mark the beginning of what she considers a downward spiral in her life. She felt there was no where to go or no one to whom she could turn. She thought the other family members knew about her plight but chose not to get involved.

Jada states,

I was too ashamed to report what was happening to me to the authorities or to my teacher.

Also, as is classic in this type of situation, Jada was protective of her mother and did not want to get her parent into trouble. Jada suffered in silence and retreated into a world of hopelessness and being voiceless.

She continues,

I didn't know what was going on. I just knew that 'Aunt' was abusive. It was not until I was almost grown before I began to realize the occurrences of brutality were related to my mother being so young when she got pregnant. She had never had a normal teen-age life. She was burdened with responsibilities and she tried to share or, at times, to escape from them.

Jada says the pain was so great that when she was about to graduate from grammar school, she, like many youngsters caught in the web of abuse and neglect, began to think of ways out of her situation. She knew if she ran away from home they would find her. She started asking her friends if they knew anyone who had committed or attempted suicide. Jada quickly told them this information was not for herself. They pointed out to her that taking an overdose of prescription drugs was one type of suicide. She decided against that method because she would not be able to control the outcome. In spite of her desire to escape her troubles, Jada did not want to kill herself. She devised a plan to drink bleach as a way of escape so that she could be taken to the hospital, not returning home. She had no idea of what might happen to her physically as a result of drinking the bleach. She would have to take that chance. She planned the event for a time when her mother was at home alone, asleep in the bedroom.

Jada remembers,

The fumes overtook me as I gasped for breath. I was so afraid. I wanted to live. I went into my mother's room and shook her. I tried talking to her but could barely get my words out. My mother was frightened. I ran to the bathroom and began vomiting. I told my mother what I wanted her to believe.

To make her actions appear to be accidental, Jada had prepared a cup of milk and a cup of bleach. The bleach was for mopping the floor. She wanted it to seem as if she accidentally drank the bleach instead of the milk. Her mother took her to the hospital where they ran tests.

I was panic stricken with the thought that my mother and my 'Aunt' might find that I intentionally drank the bleach. When I was asked by the physician to explain what happened, I felt I had no choice other than to convince him that drinking the bleach was an accident. I don't think the doctor really believed me. He asked another doctor to come in and ask me the same questions. I knew it was to see if I would repeat the same story. How could I really tell them the truth? They would not understand my reasoning, or so I thought. My unspoken cry for help, yet again, was not heard. The physician, who found no damage, sent me home.

I would often entertain the thought of committing suicide by jumping into water as I crossed bridges on foot or in cars. Something unexplainable kept me from doing so. I also had a recurring dream of falling down through an elevator, but I would always wake up before hitting the bottom.

We look at little children and think they don't know what is going on in their homes. Children are keenly aware of tensions and nuances around them, though they may say nothing.

She recalls being eleven when her family moved to another neighborhood on the southside.

I would sit on the bed at night and listen to a radio station at midnight when the song "Father, Open Our Eyes" played. I would cry. I wasn't reading the Bible and I did not have a relationship with God at that time. I attended church of another denomination, although I had been exposed to Catholicism through school. What I understood about church was, 'let's get the shout on' and things of that nature.

I, also, remember Marvin Gaye's song, 'Whats Going On' He sang about war and other conditions that were going on in the world. Even though I knew nothing about intercessory prayer at that time, I would cry out for God to help me. 'Lord, where are You?' I felt a burden for people because of the cruelty going on in the world. Of course, I was going through a lot of pain myself. I was feeling rejected, not understanding why the rest of family didn't rescue me.

A friend, whose mother worked with "Aunt", told her that Aunt and her mother were lovers. Jada was thirteen at that time. In their absences, she began to search through their belongings and to find explicit pictures and sexual devices. With what little she knew about same sex relationships, she developed a dislike for her mother and did not want her to touch her. She felt her mother was "nasty." The reality of homosexuality was further evidenced in the lifestyle of Jada's play uncle, a music teacher and weekend hairdresser. He lived across the hall and did Jada's hair in exchange for her waking him each morning. When Jada would come across the hall with keys to his apartment, she would approach his bedroom with caution and peek around the corner before entering. It was not unusual to find him asleep in the bed, naked or with a man. One morning, he was nude and tied to a rail with a rope. His apartment had been robbed. Jada says,

Loosed

*I was very frightened and ran to get 'Aunt.'
From that time on I did not have to wake 'Uncle.'
He later died from AIDS. Of course, back then, it
was hush, hush - - something that brought shame.*

Jada seldom went outside because of how she felt about
her home situation.

*I was embarrassed by the way 'Aunt' dressed
and behaved. I felt that everyone else also knew
what was going on in my household.*

The lady called "Aunt" cussed like a sailor and would
periodically drive down the street, keeping an eye on Jada. Jada
cringes as she says,

*I vividly remember an occasion when a man
tried to rape my sister as she was taking a shortcut
through a gangway. 'Aunt' chased him and shot
him in the leg as he tried to scale a fence and get
away. The incident was never reported.*

The violation of her sister's curfew on the night of her
high school graduation resulted in the sister being put out of the
house. Jada was thirteen at the time. Shortly after that incident,
Jada's mother and her lover ended their relationship, and the
mother moved in with another female lover. Jada noticed a

pattern – all of the lovers seemed to be substitute mother figures. Jada breathed a sigh of relief as she states,

> *Finally, I felt some relief because the physical and verbal abuse ended. With less fear for my safety, I turned my attention to boys. I found myself drawn to older men without giving any thought to the ramifications.*

Jada learned at an early age the price of love was too often pain. Jada recalls one such experience,

> *I met a man who provided the attention I craved; and on the second date we had sex. I became pregnant. I was in denial until I became sick and had to be taken to the hospital. My mother was hurt and my response to disappointing her was to wrap myself in the arms of two old friends – shame and rejection. I was given the choice of having the baby or an abortion. Without really weighing the options, I emerged from the arms of shame and rejection long enough to have an abortion.*

When Jada was seventeen her mother finally got an apartment of her own. The chance for the two of them to spend time together was short-lived, however. Jada wanted to go to a party, and her mother told her if she went to the party she better find some other place to live. With many young people, a dare is as good as an invitation. Jada says,

> *I went to the party and that was the last time I would live with my mother. When I returned home that night, I slept on the outside hall stairs. The next morning my mother let me into the house to get my clothes and that was it! This reinforced my long-felt sense that my mother did not want me.*
>
> *Although I had disobeyed her, I felt I was not a bad child. I was getting good grades in school and working four nights a week and giving my mother money on bills. On Saturday mornings I had to remain in the house in case my mother needed something from the store. I always made at least one trip to the store every Saturday.*

Jada recalls her mother did not have anyone in her life during this time. Her weekend drinking was increasing. Perhaps, Jada's mother felt some of the despair that often comes when one feels unloved and unworthy. These were certainly feelings Jada knew well in her own young life. Sometimes the adult and the child reverse roles. Jada's memory is filled to the brim with experiences that indicate that she was the adult and her mother the child.

It was nothing to come home and find cigarette burns on the furniture, food cooking on the stove and my mother sleeping. My mother would repeat this type of behavior over and over.

Jada makes peace with the reality of her childhood when she says,

There are such things as generational curses where the   sins of the forefathers are heaped upon the children. But with God's guidance, I feel I have overcome those curses that have come down from both parents and their ancestors.

Her reflection continues,

I could go two months without seeing my mother without feelings of guilt. I don't want to say I hated my mother, but often there is a thin line between love and hate. I think about those early days when she neither protected me nor showed me affection. There were no hugs and kisses. All I thought about was, 'Why is there no one for me? Why do I have to suffer?' She severed ties with her mother.

In spite of the tumultuous early years, Jada remained in school. At seventeen, she was a junior in high school and, with

37

her wits, negotiated living space wherever she could. Sometimes, she lived with the families of friends, her sister and her family, and spent a short time with her biological aunt.

She was on her own with no one to lean on. All sense of security was gone. She felt as long as she did what others wanted she could stay with them. The moment she did not please them or have money to give them, she knew she would be looking for another place to live. Jada recalls the first place she lived after being put out of her mother's house,

I had a girlfriend who befriended me in high school. Her mother allowed me to come and live with them until I completed high school. I shared clothing and whatever food that came into the house. Her mother taught me how to become more ladylike. She put me in a debutante cotillion and showed unconditional love. There were other friends with whom I lived. But when they got tired of me, I had to look for another place to live. I lived with my sister, her husband and two children. They lived in an area far from public transportation so my brother-in-law sold me their car. I worked evenings and attended school during the day. Eventually, the car broke down and because of the distance, I had to find a place to live closer to public transportation.

Monica Young-Freeman

Jada, in all of her struggles, not only completed high school but also enrolled in college. She had to seek full-time employment, eventually, so that she could get her own apartment. School became more than she could handle at this time. She dropped out of college. She explains,

> *My first apartment was a studio with a full-sized mattress -- no box springs -- on the floor. I used a cardboard box as a nightstand. I had one lamp, two plates, two knives and forks, and two glasses, a telephone and a black and white television. Jada knew firsthand what it was like to do without and to live from place to place.*

During a period when she collected unemployment benefits, Jada was able to pay rent, utilities and treat herself to the movies twice a month. Yes, her spirit always remained high. Jada recalls the small church in which she grew up as a place where she found some comfort. She recalls her experience and that this church was not without its problems. The membership was predominantly women and children.

> *There were not many male role models. Many of the men in the church acted like 'Uncle,' and I saw older men 'turnout' (introduce homosexuality) young boys. Before 'Aunt' left, we attended this particular church as a family. She would tell us*

some of the secrets of some of the women mem-bers of this church. Although they were married, they were trying out the homosexual lifestyle or experience. They came to our house to play cards without their husbands.

This was the place where our gay choir direc-tor later introduced me to a well-known, married minister from another state. During the course of our relationship, the minister told me that he cared about me, and that he and his wife were only together for the sake of the church and media. He cared enough about her not to humiliate her.

Our church visited his church, and I remember his wife coming to introduce herself to me. I could not believe it! He had told her about me! I was drawn to his lifestyle, his popularity and the atten-tion he gave me. When it came to our sexual inti-macy, I did not particularly like having sex with him. I had decided if this was what I had to do to feel loved and special, I would go along with it.

Jada reports that whenever the minister came to town, other ministers would meet at his hotel room. She saw them exchanging sermons and some were smoking marijuana. Jada remembers going to visit some of the churches where her minis-ter friend was guest preacher. She saw women flocking to him even though he did not give them his attention. This made Jada feel even more special because, though he was married, he would give his attention to only her. There was something within her, however, that would not allow her to be comfortable with this situation. She says,

I knew my teachings from the Bible. Therefore, I knew this was not right. The relationship ended. Looking back, I believe part of the reason I experienced a confused situation, such as this, was because I was trying to make it on my own without knowing the spiritual consequences of my behavior. How could I, when there had been no one to teach me? Yet, I knew right from wrong.

Jada believes the church of her youth planted the seed for her spiritual path. She says,

I was in church but I still didn't have a relationship with the Lord. I was on my own, with no one to answer to, and I would leave church to go to my boyfriend's house. I always remembered to go to church on Sundays. This was what I knew. I thought this was a way of life.

In this dysfunctional family, the inevitable losses mounted. These losses included her innocence, the normal ebb and flow and childhood discoveries, a sense of trust, and the ability to know love as an unconditional right of childhood. The strong sense of survival that seemed to be embedded in her had protected her from the wounds created by the adults in her life. It took years for some of the unhealed wounds to heal.

It is so important to have a sense of the person to whom we commit our lives in marriage. So much can be hidden behind the fire of lust and under the veil of respectability while marriage provides for our desire to express our mutual love. Sometimes, appearances like beauty, are skin-deep. Beyond seeming to be one who served God and worshiped the ground she walked on, Jada had no knowledge as to the depth of Judas's soul. It began to be clear to her that being an object of a man's worship was not really the answer to filling the void left from never knowing unconditional love.

Chapter 2

THE UNHEALED WOUND

The wounds of the body may be deep
But the wounds of the soul are deeper still

Reflecting on her adolescent and teen years, Jada describes herself,

I was sexually promiscuous as I desperately searched for love. I had no past role models that taught me how to be the giver or receiver of love. As far back as I can remember, I knew about the importance of love rather than having its actual presence in my life. Every part of me cried out for the touch and words of those who might love me. The closest I came to receiving unconditional love was when I was with my sister, maternal aunt and cousins. Outwardly, emotional expressions and moments of touching were the types of love I saw displayed. As a young woman, my body became the way to attract what I thought was love.

I was drawn to older men who seemed to be established. I was not interested in school sports, nor did I have an interest in proms. I'm not sure why I was unconcerned with most things young

girls my age would have found interesting. I can only think it was because I was growing up too fast and had already been exposed to worldly conditions too soon. I remember lying to my mother about my high school prom photos. I didn't attend my high school prom.

Instead, I chose to go to an adult party being held downtown. You were suppose to be at least twenty-one to get in. Of course, my girl friend and I knew how to get around that barrier. I felt twenty-one because of my life's exposures. As I look back, I regret all of those lost moments of not experiencing normal teen and adolescent fun.I can remember my mother saying, on several occasions, to me, 'You are going to have the rest of your life to be grown. You need to try to stay a child as long as you can.' I had a mind of my own, however, and was moving fast.

I traveled and met people who seemed to like me and to treat me nice, but I soon discovered that appearances can be deceiving and unrealistic. Drugs and other dangers lurked in the shadows of what seemed, on the surface, to be exotic living. How did I escape the pitfalls of this world? I learned early to resist anything that controlled me. Although I tried drugs in high school, I didn't like the feeling of anything taking over and controlling me. Therefore, I chose not to pursue controlled *substances as a means of escaping reality. I remember two bad incidents when I experimented with chemical substances. Once, someone gave me a downer. I took it while at school. Within a half an hour, I was nodding in one of my classes. Having a teacher with a compassionate heart kept me from getting into a lot of trouble. She allowed me to sleep off the drug in the back of the room.*

The second incident was with an older man. I thought I liked him and I thought he liked me. Being in high school, I was really impressed with him. He was sophisticated and had many material possessions. In his presence, I felt special. I was living with a friend and her mother at the time, basically on my own. This older man was a teacher who also sold drugs. He offered me some of the "happening" drug of those times, cocaine. Instead, it turned out to be speed. I'll never forget the experience. I began to think I was in the middle of Lake Michigan and on a spinning spindle, going around and around. I thought, at any moment, I was going to fall off and drown. He took advantage of me sexually, then called my girl friend. She and her boyfriend gave me baking soda to make me vomit and to cleanse the drug out of my system. It seems as though I stayed high for two days. After this experience, I felt violated.

As I think over my life, I can only say God was

and has been with me, and, certainly, I know He has had a purpose for my life! In spite of myself, I'm amazed at all He has brought me through.

Jada's adolescent experiences include marriage. She says,

At age eighteen, I met the man who became my first husband, after some years of being together. He was eleven years my senior, had his own condominium, drove a nice car and respected me. We dated until I was twenty-seven. I wanted to get married, but he would continue to put marriage off. He had been married and had children. Marriage held no mystery for him. He was the first man who showed me any commitment in a relationship. He came from a home where his mother and father were always there for him. Year after year, he promised me that next year, we would marry. Eventually, I became weary and started to have interests outside this relationship. I felt I had made myself available, giving my body, time and opening up my entire life to him. I suppose he thought I was not going anywhere. Therefore, he could take his time, have some fun, and when he got tired, he would marry me.

Meanwhile, I met someone else in whom I was interested. This other man and I were close in age. I liked him and told him that I was dating someone. He didn't seem to mind. I suppose he felt that if I had dated someone for eight years, and had not married, there must not be anything there. Further proof was, I was talking to him, the younger man.

In spite of what Jada describes as promiscuous behavior, her character reflected a certain level of personal integrity. She reports,

As time went on, I found myself still drawn to the younger man. I did not want to 'cheat.' I decided to tell my future husband I had met someone else. My older friend assumed, since I had been with him for so long, I was never going anywhere. He was very surprised at my news and was suddenly ready to get married. My long-time, older friend insisted that I choose between the two. I chose him, the older man. Speaking of marrying for all of the wrong reasons, here was a perfect example. My rationale was I had already spent so many years with him and the other relationship was new. I didn't really know the younger man and stood to lose more if I chose him.

Loosed

We agreed to marry in six months. When I informed the younger man, he asked, 'Why is he now ready to marry you?' I remember thinking 'I could have married him a long time ago if I had made him think there was someone else.'

Jada saw a physician, explaining that she did not enjoy sex, and wanted to be examined to see if she had a problem. She knew her desires were for men and knew what an orgasm felt like. Her friends would tell her how wonderful it felt when they experienced sex while she had always faked orgasms. Jada says,

Once while having sex with my husband and faking an orgasm, he said, 'Stop. I know you are not having an orgasm.' I was so embarrassed. I would play games such as waiting for him to go to sleep, then come to bed. Or pretend to be asleep when he would come to bed. Or say 'I'm so tired.'

In spite of her efforts to be contented in her marriage, Jada reports being very "bored." They were living in an apartment above his mother's. Jada discovered the downside of being in a close-knit family. She wanted them to have a place of their own, but her husband was more comfortable with things as they were. Jada's mother-in-law depended on her son to do things around the house. Jada says,

It was not the fact of him helping his mother. It was that I felt I had to compete for his time. Also, I felt I was being compared with his mother. If I did not cook, she would cook for him. If he needed something washed, she would do it. It became clear to me that we didn't need to live in the same house with his mother.

In time, they both stopped putting effort into the marriage. The saying, "An idle mind is the devil's workshop" became a reality in her marriage.

Eventually, Jada and her husband separated. They continued to communicate and discovered they missed one another. They talked about reconciling. Jada came to the conclusion that what she felt for her husband was paternal love or love of a daughter for a father. Jada reports the following,

I felt alone and detached. The feelings I had were not romantic ones, but my husband made me feel loved. We did reconcile, however, and moved back together. Although the marriage did not last, I have remained friends with him and his mother. I was finally able to put my love for him into perspective. I loved him like a family member.

Jada had an image of what marriage should be. She envisioned the type of fulfilling relationship she wanted. She did this, though there were no positive role models of a successful marriage in her family. Consequently, how could she have anything other than misconceptions? She wanted to be married to keep from sinning, and, equally important, she wanted to be truly loved.

> *I thought, God, I want a man who will worship the ground I walk on, one who is in the church.*

She has since learned the lesson, "Be careful for what you ask, you may receive it!"

Jada had been gone from her old church for some time. When she found herself back, she thought,

> *Who would have thought I would return to the church where I grew up. I hadn't been there for a number of years. A friend who still attended invited me to the church's annual choir concert.*

Jada recalls that she was enjoying the concert when a man entered and sat next to her.

> *I noticed him because of his distinguished look. He was well dressed and his skin was dark and smooth. As he sat down, he spoke to me and I acknowledged him. At intermission, he started a*

50

conversation in which he explained how he happened to attend the concert.

She had prayed for a man involved in the church. The man sitting next to her mentioned his church membership. Jada says,

His church, the pastor and its choir were well-known. I had visited his church on several occasions. As we talked, his body language indicated that he was attracted to me, but I played it off. I was trying to focus on my reason for the visit to my old church. I did find him attractive, but a relationship with him did not enter my mind. After the concert ended, I went to use the pay phone inside the church and noticed he was standing outside the building. I later found out that he was waiting for me to leave the church so that he could talk to me. As I walked toward my car, I did not see him. Another man greeted me and introduced himself as Reverend Whatever. I was surprised because I thought I was going to run into Judas. I was polite to the minister, but not interested. As we talked, I noticed that Judas was making it obvious he was waiting patiently for me. He was leaning against a black imported car. Finally, the Reverend picked up on this. I turned and asked Judas if he was waiting for me? My intent was to end the conversation with the Reverend. I knew him slightly from a

51

previous visit to the church and didn't want to hurt his feelings.

Although I exchanged telephone numbers with Judas, I didn't intend to call him. He was not my type and, from the conversation, it seemed we had little in common, other than church because my lifestyle had caused me to be more exposed much sooner. I decided that if he called I would go out to dinner with him. Perhaps, we could, also, share our spiritual walk by attending each other's churches.

Looking back, Jada says,

Our first feelings are often the Holy Spirit directing us. These feelings should not be ignored. He called shortly after our first encounter at the church. I was bored and lonely so I decided to go on a date with him. In the back of my mind, it still bothered me that we had so little in common. I shared with a girl friend, 'He's so polite and attentive. No one else has ever treated me this way!' I loved it, but decided I was not attracted to him in other ways. My girl friend replied, 'Girl, if he is treating you nice and giving you attention, don't worry about the other things. They'll grow on you.'
I begin justifying why I should continue to see

him. The rationale was that I needed to get used to dating a church person. I was not used to his kind of treatment. Other men I had known were from outside the church. Also, I had asked God to send me a Godly husband. I had also asked for one who worshiped the ground I walked on. Was God answering my prayer?

Weeks became months, we dated and we discussed sex. Judas knew I had very strong feelings about following God's way, this time around. I didn't want to repeat the pattern I followed in my first marriage. It was important to me that we enter into this relationship the right way, God's way. He agreed. After six months, we married.

She begins to talk about the unfolding of the drama of getting to know Judas.

I didn't know the family of Judas too well. I only knew he had been married while in the military and had a son. He had extreme introverted behavior, and I thought maybe that was why he spent so much time up under me. There were times I wanted to do things with my friends that excluded him. He took this as a rejection. I had to constantly reassure him of my love for him. I suggested that he do things with his friends, and discovered he had no friends. I didn't think much of it at the time. Our biggest battles were concerned with his wanting to spend more time with me after marrying I began to feel I had no life outside our marriage. He became resentful of my friends, and didn't want to be excluded from the group, even during after-church fellowship. People began to ask me if Judas disliked them. My friends were uncomfortable on the occasions we went out together. Judas began to physically block my leaving home, take my car keys and follow me and then demand that I leave with him. Since I didn't like to create a scene, his tactics worked at first. When I asked him why he picked verbal fights, his reply was he didn't know exactly why. He said there was something about my breaking down and crying and then our making

up that he liked. After one of those episodes, there would be three to seven days of honeymoon. Then the cycle would begin again. His mood swings were also affected by problems he had with his co-workers. Sometimes, when he was upset, he would take the money that was to be used to pay the bills and shop for clothes. I had the responsibility for the apartment and utilities because they were in my name.

He had qualities that other women wished their husbands had. He cooked, cleaned, washed and shopped for groceries. On the other hand, he thought I was his property. He seemed to want to love me but had deep insecurities. To try to lessen those insecurities, I told him why I loved him. I told him that one of his features that appealed to me was his beautiful dark skin. I would stroke his face and rub his hair to reassure him of my love. As a child he was teased and called 'Blackie.' He was a short man and I think his height added to his lack of confidence. I later discovered that no one else had ever shown him the kind of unconditional love I had given him.

Judas began to open up more, as much as he could, and talk about his childhood and his relationships with his parents. He was raised in the Holiness Church. As a child his activities were greatly restricted. Swimming, basketball and other sports, engaged in by many young people, were viewed as sins. His mother was the more dominant parent while the father was soft-spoken and retiring. Judas joined the marines to get away from his home life. He also married at this time. When his marriage ended, he returned home. He had always lived at home except during his marriage and his military stint. Here again, I had married a man who lived in his parent's home.

As long as I did what he wanted, there were no problems. The trouble began when I told him my feelings of being unhappy, controlled and smoth-

ered. At first, his response was to leave home at night and not return until the next morning. He was driving around, he said. This didn't bother me, because, instead of arguing all night, I could get some rest.

Then his behavior changed. He would speed home from work and wait for me to arrive. I would have to explain why I was late. I looked forward to going to work and to Friday night prayer service. Otherwise, I dreaded the weekends. I looked forward to Sundays since we attended different churches. I was free to be me.

I started leaving town when he became angry and only returned home when I thought he had calmed down. He repeatedly promised to control his anger and rage. He would blame his mood swings on being a diabetic. The rage would escalate, and, at times, he would stand over me or pin me down. His facial expressions seemed demonic. I believed his explanations for the outbursts, at first. When I questioned other diabetics, they didn't experience similar feelings or experiences. My pleas for him to see a doctor or a counselor fell on deaf ears. Finally, I asked for a divorce.

After the divorce he continued to call. He also told me, he was getting counseling and had no one to whom he felt he could turn. I wanted to believe him, and, also, thought I should be getting counsel-

ing. I had mixed emotions. On the one hand, I feared him and felt he would never leave me alone. On the other hand, I felt sorry for him. To be truthful, I did not really want to be alone. I did not want to start over again, and I did not like the feeling I had failed at this marriage. This was a time further complicated by my mother being diagnosed with terminal lung cancer. I was trying to be strong for her and for my family. I was taking my mother back and forth to her chemotherapy sessions. My work as a consultant was coming to an end. On top of my being concerned about my mother, I was about to have financial problems. I walked around as if everything was fine. I functioned at work. When I attended intercessory prayer meetings, this was the one place I felt I could cry out to God. I didn't believe my family understood what I was feeling because they were busy dealing with Mama's illness. In the meantime, he was constantly there, pleading for another chance. One truth about having a victim mentality is the longer you stay in this frame of mind, the weaker you become. It's the same as having a python sucking the life out of you. Eventually, you die, either -- spiritually, emotionally, mentally or physically. Initially, I would sneak to see him, because I was ashamed of accepting him back. Others had witnessed much of what I had been through and I certainly remem-

bered my trauma. I thought I was strong, but I was not. I deceived myself into believing things would be better if we reconciled. Why? Was it because I didn't want to be alone? Was I more vulnerable because of the cares of the world that weighed on me during this period of my life? Or was it simply because of the negative relationship pattern I had experienced most of my life? I still wanted to be loved without knowing real love.

When Jada remarried her second husband, she recalls the word of a well-known gospel song sung during the ceremony, "Have you done what I have asked of you?" Jada says,

I remember crying. Those around me thought these were tears of happiness. I was not at peace, and knew I should not have remarried my second husband. Again, my reasoning was wrong. I wanted to prove to others that God could restore a marriage. I didn't want anyone to know how I felt because I had unrealistic expectations of my self and this relationship. I thought my fears were a sign of weakness. I would often ask myself, 'How can I be an intercessor for someone else and believe God will answer his or her prayer while not having faith in God restoring my marriage?

A friend later told Jada that perhaps God had answered her prayer. She did not hear the answer because Jada heard what she wanted to hear, not what God was telling her.

My friend's statement remains with me. I now realize that there were many times when I think the answer to my prayers is not the will of God. Since God is all knowing, He knows the beginning and the end. I was justifying what was happening and sometimes even thought I was suppose to suffer. I believed Judas would see God in me, and, thereby, he would change. As I prayed to heal my victim mentality, I came to imagine myself in my mother's place and could finally see the good things she had done for me. As I emptied my heart in my prayers before God, I would hear God saying, 'There is no condemnation.' God was right there with open arms forgiving her and washing away her sins just as He forgave and washed away mine. As I went, I was healed.

At this point in her story, Jada goes back to a memory from her early twenties. Her mother joined the army to become an operating-room technician. It was during her mother's two-year tour of army duty when a change began to take place between her mother and herself.

Loosed

My mother asked me to visit her on the army base. She showed me off to her military friends. I was moved by how proud she was to say I was her daughter. Mother was always proud of my sister, but I had never seen this display of affection openly expressed for me. She seemed genuinely concerned about me and would write letters and send me money. It even appeared that she wanted a relationship with me.

Jada recalls how good this made her feel.

My mother was no longer drinking the way she had in the past. When she completed her army enlistment and returned home, our relationship continued. We had more family contacts. I slowly began to reciprocate her affection.

For Jada, there was also a recall of the childhood images of other parents and families kissing their children. Throughout her life, Jada had longed for this for herself.

Jada says,

I began to initiate the desired contact by kissing my mother on the cheek. My mother felt uncomfortable, at first, but I continued until she began to kiss me whenever we parted. I also started to share my personal life with her, but events of my childhood remained unspoken. Occasionally, when the past was brought up at family gatherings, my mother would deny or say she did not remember. I believe those recollections were too painful for her to talk about. I accepted this and only talked about the good things that happened in the early years of my adolescence. From this point on, whenever I was sick, my mother was there. She even attended my high school graduation.

Jada remembers the event that stands out among all other encounters with her mother, the sharing of Jada receiving of the Holy Spirit. Her mother wanted to receive the Holy Spirit. It was not long after Jada's experience that her mother became a member of Jada's church and, indeed, received the Holy Spirit herself. The barrier that blocked the relationship between mother and daughter was finally rolled away as were Jada's concerns about her mother's spiritual health. Her mother's physical health deteriorated and she had to be hospitalized often.

Jada says,

I knew that if my mother had a personal relationship with God, my worries about her health would decrease. I often reflect, with thanksgiving, over God reconciling us, and for our fifteen years as spiritually grounded mother and daughter.

Loosed

Adolescence, in and of itself, is a time of confusion. The yin and yang that naturally balance us pulls us apart at the same time. The understanding necessary to critically examine choices before acting is not yet available to the average young person. When the drama combines with hormones raging out of control, the adolescent is often stretched beyond capacity. When this difficult-to-control time is coupled with parents who are stuck in adolescence, the family is unable to provide the balance needed for the young person to develop into a mentally, physically, emotionally and spiritually healthy adult. Without intervention, the wounds from childhood are carried throughout life.

Chapter 3

A TIME FOR KNOWING AND CHANGING

*The time for the harvesting of the seeds that
are planted deeply into the soul of even the
most remote person comes in due season.*

Catholicism was the religion practiced before "Aunt" came into Jada's life and that of her family. She attended Catholic grammar school and mass. "Aunt" had a godmother who was a member of a Baptist church to which the family was invited. Eventually, this became the family church. From the ages of nine to twenty-three, Jada attended this church. In her search she found herself exploring other churches and non-Christian religions as well. She went through a period where she pierced her nose and stopped straightening her hair. She called it her "African Thing." In spite of her explorations, the seeds were planted deep, and she continued to stand in Christianity.

As a young adult, she finds her new church and becomes very active there. She works in the prayer room with people who are praying to receive the Holy Spirit. She has such a desire to pray with others. This is so, because it has troubled her when she has found herself in past religious experiences that did not include the Holy Spirit. She knew she was saved but realized there was still something missing. She had not yet experienced the free-flowing experience of speaking in an unknown tongue.

She becomes involved in the church's outreach ministry and travels to areas where crime and drugs are prevalent. She distributes food and tells passing people, who would listen, about Jesus and salvation. Jada also becomes involved in the prison ministry. She remembers,

> *This area of ministry was the most difficult for me. I did not have a desire to become apart of the prison ministry. I had promised to participate in this ministry and made a commitment to do so because it was part of the outreach program. I felt compassion for those on the street because, though I had never been homeless, I knew about surviving at an early age.*
>
> *We go to the maximum security block where the inmates are being held. I feel very uncomfortable with the types of looks I am receiving from the men. I am always very careful about the clothes I wear, making sure they are not too tight, short or seductive. There is an episode during one visit when I am told I will lead the prayer. We have a female chaplain who dresses as a nun would dress. She tells the minister that she does not want me to*

lead the prayer because I have a slit in my skirt. I am embarrassed and hurt. The slit is at the bottom of my skirt. Given the way I ordinarily dressed, I am definitely stripped down. My attitude is I didn't want to look as if I were a nun.

Jada learns that you sometimes must put your feelings aside and do things you don't want to do in order to witness to others about God. Jada finally decides it is time to leave prison ministry after a trip to the tiers of inmates who were either on bad behavior or had elected not to come down to the gym where the services were being held.

She explains,

During my last visit, we were standing in front of a cell and one of the inmates keeps trying to make eye contact with me. I never look directly at him because I am aware of what he is trying to do. During the course of praying and reading the word of God, I position myself behind some of the ministers. That meant the inmate cannot see me. He repositions himself by moving to the other side of the cell, where he could see me. He appears to be fantasizing about me. This makes me feel violated. I then accept I am not cut out for this type of ministry.

Loosed

At Jada's old church, she sees herself as one who, in the past, has avoided expressing outward emotions while attending church. Others might cry, shout and dance, but not Jada. She's always concerned about how others perceive her. She describes the strong inward emotions she had been experiencing.

In spite of appearances, I feel the presence of God. My teeth begin to clatter against each other and my tongue moves in an uncontrollable fashion. I think at first I am developing a nervous condition.

Jada puts her hand over her mouth. While listening to religious radio, she begins to understand what is happening to her. The radio hosts speak about the Holy Spirit and speaking in tongues. Perhaps, most important to Jada,

If you don't have the Holy Spirit, you are not saved! I know I am saved; but if there were tongues to be given through the Holy Spirit, I so want this experience.

At that time, her church did not address or preach about speaking in tongues. This topic was only brought up when there was a discussion of the Upper Room or Azusa.

Monica Young-Freeman

Jada says,

I have a hunger for more Jesus and begin to visit churches throughout the week I hear on the radio. I become angry because no one has church on Saturday.

Jada recalls a Sunday when she overhears another choir member talking about a church that believes in the fulfilling of the Holy Spirit with evidence of speaking in tongues. This church is also described as having a ministry that focuses on deliverance. She finds herself intrigued by what she overhears, interrupting to ask for the name and location. She visits the church on a weeknight, not knowing anyone. There are deliverance services on Mondays and Fridays. She sees the same two women, who had been talking, at the rear of this church. She goes over to the women and tells them she has heard someone say, "If you have not spoken in tongues, you are not saved."

She tells them, "I know I am saved, but I desire to speak in tongues."

The women do not condemn her. Instead, they tell her, "We are going to touch and agree with you." They hold her hands, tell her to open her mouth and begin to praise God. "Don't worry about what comes out of your mouth," they say. Jada continues her description. It is clear that she is reliving a time that has had a great impact on her.

67

Loosed

Suddenly unknown words begin to flow abundantly out of my mouth. I am so overtaken. These women show only love for one who is a stranger. This is miraculous!

Jada will never forget the ride home. No one is in the car with her. Her speaking in tongues continues.

I don't want to stop. People driving past look as if they think I am strange, but I don't care. I want to open the windows and tell them what I have just experienced. I am on fire.

Since Jada's relationship with her mother has changed, her first thought, when she gets home, is to call her and tell her to come over. The next day before Jada can get in the house, her mother and her friend are standing in the hall. As she is trying to tell them what has happened to her, her tongues change. She tries to stop and control her words because she doesn't want them to think she is trying to show off.

I am not in control of this experience. My mother looks at me intensely. She knows this is real and her eyes fill with tears. This is a turning point for me. My spirituality has been taken to a new level. My mother and my sister are both impacted by this.

Jada begins to attend both the family church and the deliverance church for two years. She reports,

I learn about spiritual warfare and getting healing for myself at the deliverance church. It is here I begin to forgive my mother, because I understand for the first time the pain she has experienced all of her life. The most important healing I welcome is I learn to forgive myself and to end my life-long relationship with shame and rejection. The shame is for the unspoken sinful acts I had committed. It is not enough to just be forgiven and to forgive; I want to know where the gift of forgiveness comes from. In addition to attending the deliverance church, I spend time with God and cry out as I read the Bible. God begins to unveil the curses that traveled from one generation to another. It also becomes clear the warfare I am encountering is spiritual – that there is a God and a Satan. God makes it clear He is our mighty high tower, and no matter how much power the prince of darkness has, God is greater than Satan.

In revealing the purpose of the Holy Spirit, God makes clear that I am not to see myself as a victim, but as an over-comer. He has given us authority over every satanic attack that awaits us. This fire shut up in my bones causes me to grow stronger day by day. Eventually, I openly praise God at all times.

Loosed

Jada is determined to tell the world there is much more to God than most have experienced. This desire to be free and witness to others, results in her restless at her old family church. She discovers she feels spiritually fed at the deliverance church. She has a particular interest in the deliverance ministry and intercessory prayer group. She witnesses to people, right before her eyes, she sees demonic manifestations. One such situation, at her family church, involves a woman who obsessively believes the pastor is her husband. The deacons have to stop her when she, believing the pastor needs her, walks toward the altar. Jada recalls a highly unusual incident.

The woman leaves the church during the service, only to return at the end of the service. The pastor calls the deacons so the group can pray for the woman. The woman and I are both in the rear of the church. The deacons encircle the pastor and the disturbed woman as the pastor prays. He touches the woman and when he removes his hand, it appears something lifts him up and slings him backwards over the last pew. The pastor gasps for air and the deacons catch him as he lands on the floor. The pastor appears to have lost consciousness. The woman seems to be normal again and waves a scarf as she praises God. No one openly talks about what has happened, but I know that a demonic spirit has been cast out of the woman. The demonic spirit had attacked the pastor.

Jada remembers visiting many churches as she is searching. She realizes that though she had a "soul tie" with her family church, something is now missing. In the search process, Jada discovers the new church where they believe in the indwelling of the Holy Spirit and baptize in the name of Jesus. At the Baptist church they baptize in the name of the Father, the Son and the Holy Ghost. Jada attends the 9:10 a.m. service so that she can get to her family church to be able to sing in the choir at 11:30 a.m. The first time she attends the new church she responds to the altar call, before knowing what she is doing. She is taken into the tarry room to pray for the indwelling of the Holy Spirit. She remembers telling them,

I already have the Holy Spirit. They say, 'Praise the Lord.' They begin to speak in tongues as I do. It feels so good to already know the power of this experience. I am also baptized again that day. I feel led by an unexplainable hunger to do what God wants.

Loosed

Jada explains further,

The Sunday I visit the church, the pastor is not even there. I learn later that he is in the hospital. I know it is neither the pastor nor the 'who's who' that causes me to walk down that aisle. I am dressed in my other church uniform and my plan is to keep this new membership a secret. No one will understand my being a member of two different churches, and, also attended the deliverance church certainly, not a church outside my denomination. I attend two churches on Sunday and a third one during the week. Others will think I am confused, but I feel so completely happy. I hope, with time, I will be able to share what I am learning with the members of my family church. Instead, I grow increasingly restless. Six months from the time I visit the new church I make the decision to leave my old family church. Needless to say, the pastor is not pleased. A member calls me on a Sunday and shares the pastor's sermon. He has preached about people who get 'older and educated and high and mighty' and decide they are not getting what they need at their old church. The pastor was then reported to have said, 'If they are not getting it here, it is because of them. It is not because I am not giving it.'

I feel hurt and rejected. I write a detailed letter to the pastor explaining why I am changing my membership. It takes a great deal of effort to not place blame on anyone for my arriving at my decision to leave the church. As time passes, I am invited by friends to attend a revival service at my old church. The pastor calls everyone down who needs healing and prays for them. It becomes clear to me that my prayers for reconciliation have been answered. Even though I haven't returned as a member of that congregation, God reconciles the relationship between the pastor and myself.

God also makes it clear I can't be in two places at the same time. I decide I can pray for the people at my former church while belonging to my new church. That is where I want to be.

Jada begins to meet once a month with a group of women who fellowship at someone's home. They talk, while eating, about problems they are having. Someone suggests that they start praying for one another. Jada sees God use this gathering to start an intercessory prayer group. During this period, Jada has divorced her first husband and married her second husband. She states,

This was the marriage I thought was the result of my prayers. I believe God has sent me a husband who is in the church and who worships the ground

73

I walk on. I think trying to remain in this marriage is drawing me closer to God. It actually takes more prayer to deal with a man who sees me as his property. In this type of situation, you either grow closer to God or go in the opposite direction. I am a prayer warrior who prays for everyone else. Therefore, I think, 'I just need to pray this thing through.' I struggle with this marital situation for two years. He is not physically violent. He restrains me, takes my keys, locks the doors, listens to my telephone calls and follows me. He thinks everyone is trying to take me away from him.

I begin to realize that I am in a crazy situation and seek help in the intercessory prayer group. We discover many others need this group into the prayer room at church. We meet on Tuesday nights and have services on Friday nights.

In the meantime, the circumstances in my life continue to require prayer. I have a disturbed husband, my mother is dying and I discover I am pregnant. Although, at times, I feel I am losing my mind, I never stop praying. If a time comes when you don't feel like praying, you keep going until you get to a place where you can feel God. Perhaps, what is most important, are the times when you can't pray. Just knowing you can call on someone who can get a prayer through makes these covenant prayer sisters and brothers invaluable. They are able to feel the problem in Spirit realm and connect with one another without having to be told what is going on. It does not matter where the saints gather to pray - - in a basement, car, conference room or a sanctuary. Wherever and whatever it takes for the prayers of the righteous to avail.

Her mother dies, but Jada, though mourning, is looking forward to having the opportunity to love a child unconditionally. Two months after her mother's death, however, there are complications. Her labor is induced and the infant is stillborn. At this point, she prays to God,

'You know what God, I no longer have to be strong for my mother. Nor do I have to be concerned about my child. I know it is not Your will for me to live like this any longer.'

This was a turning point for Jada in her marriage. She told Judas she was divorcing him. His response,

'If you divorce me, you will be sorry. You are going to pay. You are going to pay.'

75

Loosed

He repeats this statement when she asks what he means. Jada files for divorce. Her thought is,

If I am going to die, I will die leaving the marriage, not while remaining in the marriage.

He later says if she gives him five hundred dollars to buy black and navy suits, he will sign the divorce papers. It turns out his plan is to decide which suit he should be buried in. He wants to look good at his funeral. Jada says,

I don't believe him. I didn't believe he is at the point where he would commit suicide. True, his behavior is crazy, but he is not the usual batterer.

According to their divorce papers, he is to move out of the house at the end of the month. She comes home after divorcing him and finds him in the house. He says to her,

You didn't think I was going to let you divorce me and I am not going to do anything to you, did you?

He then goes to the back of the house and comes back with a pair of black gloves, along with something Jada can not see. He places the object under the couch pillow, saying,

You are going to pay. How do you want to die?
Do you want me to cut you up into little pieces?
No, I won't do that because you will look bad at the
funeral. I'll strangle you.

Jada can't believe his words and her mind can't comprehend what is happening. She is thinking, it is like something out of a movie. She says,

It couldn't be happening to me. 'If you are
going to kill me, why make me suffer? If you want
me to die, give me some medicine or something.
You don't have to make me suffer,' I struggle to
speak.

He has recently undergone surgery and has some medication left. He decides to give her the remaining pills. Jada is scared to run for fear he has a gun and will shoot her. She did not know what he has put under the pillow on the couch. He feeds her the pills. She begins to feel drowsy. He says,

'No, I don't think I want you to die. I am going
to call the hospital.'

He calls the hospital to ask for the treatment of overdosing on the medicine. His behavior becomes even more bizarre. He says to her, as she reclines on the couch,

77

Loosed

'No, Jada. I don't want you to die. Tomorrow, we are going to City Hall and remarry. No one is going to know that you divorced me.'

Jada decides she is no longer dealing with demons but with Satan himself. She says,

Since you don't have a visit from Satan every day, it is difficult to know how to respond. All I could repeat was, 'The blood of Jesus, the blood of Jesus.'

The bleach strategy from her childhood rushes into her mind as she thinks,

'Perhaps, I can take enough of the remaining medicine to make me pass out at City Hall. I'll be taken to the hospital to escape this situation.'

As in childhood, Jada says,

I don't want to die, but I don't want to remarry this man. So I say to him, 'I can't take this any longer. I don't want to live.' However, my pleas fall on deaf ears. I go to the bathroom and get the bottle and hide it. My hope is I will collapse at City Hall and end up in the hospital. My plan doesn't work. He completes the necessary papers and, as

78

crazy as I must have looked, no one notices. On the way home, I tell him I had taken another type of medicine. He replies, 'Oh, Jada, you can not die. If you commit suicide you know you are going to hell.' In my mind, I am thinking, 'This is the craziest stuff I have ever heard in my life.'

Instead of taking me to the hospital, he takes me to a restaurant. After arriving home, the medicine is beginning to work. He tries to keep me awake. He still can't risk taking me to the hospital, because I might tell someone what has happened. There was no food in the house, and he, being a diabetic, needs to eat. He puts the telephone near the couch and reminds me that I am not going to die. He tells me to call my godmother, if I must, while he goes out to get some groceries. Once he leaves, I call my godmother who calls others, and they take me to the hospital and, later, to the police.

Now, I am in hiding, afraid to go to work. Finally, I decide I am not running any longer. He calls me at work, from a New York City parking garage, and tells me he is attending a church revival. He says he is getting ready to kill himself. At that moment, it seems my prayers have not been heard. He has made a decision not to surrender his life to the Lord. The stain of sin would be upon him. It is clear to me that he wishes to harm me, but I don't believe he will try to kill me. My thought, in that brief moment, was I wish he would hurry up if he is going to kill himself. A terrible thought to hold but I am terrified and growing weaker. I wish he would just do it.

Chapter 4

AND YET WE RISE

*The lessons we learn during our
journey on this earth are not about us,
but about glorifying God.
Outcomes that are good, bad or indifferent,
still require us to give the glory for
our being to God.*

Jada reflects on her shared story and wonders about what she may be omitting. She describes her feelings on this particular morning,

I arose this morning with an unsettled feeling, a sense of not being at peace. Telling my story in this book is troubling me. Many thoughts have raced through my mind. I know that it is the Holy Spirit. I'm crying even as I write this in my diary. I'm frightened because it's so important that I tell God's story. Only He must get the GLORY. If only a handful of people read this book, the truth must be told with no thought of what it will mean for me if others know of my pain. God must get the credit. Lord, how can I share my life and, at the same time, not feel free to deal with the truth. Truth is my spirit. No, it's not a pretty picture, but this is who I was and am. Yes, it is hard to write this book.

Loosed

I have fears of failure; fears of what others will think of me; fears of what my husband will think of me. I would like to be accepted by everyone, but that is not realistic. That is not life. It will never happen.

Jada turns to me and expresses her doubts.

Are you able to write words that will capture the intensity of my pain on paper? I don't expect you to feel my pain. You were not there, nor have you experienced the things I have. Yet, as I sit here, I am convinced that my being used as a human sacrifice, my suffering, is the will of the Father.

She then moans,

Pain, pain, pain! Though the remembering and the telling of my story is painful, it is the sacrifice I must make to be set free! I am free when I can share and cry out to God. He already knows me and all about my faults, my insecurities and my Challenges - - all of my weaknesses. I am reminded of a singer who wrote the words of a song saying, 'What if I ask you to give up the very thing that you love, would you still serve Me (God)? What if it costs you your life? Would you still serve me?' The answer for me is, 'Yes, God.'

We have all made decisions we know are wrong and, at the time, hope no one will ever find out. There is still another side to this removing of the silence and crying out. This is a way of rejoicing. How does it feel when you come out of the wilderness? There is a biblical verse that makes it very plain. Then you will know the truth, and the truth will set you free. John 8:32 (NIV). The Holy Spirit has convinced me, as much as I want this book to be written and to reach all lives, it is intended to fall into the hands of those God wants to minister.

It appears that instead of talking to me, Jada is working out the direction she is receiving from the Holy Spirit, as to the shape our project is to take. For the first time, the power that is in part of the title, **As I Went, I Was Healed,** becomes clear to me. It seems as Jada comes to grips with her own doubt about the direction of the book, she seems perfectly confident. She then lowers her head and returns her attention to me, speaking as if all questions have been removed.

You ask me the question, do I want the book to be religious, spiritual or secular? My response is I want God to be mentioned, because He was my Savior through it all. With this direction, if some professor of education or a psychologist wishes to use this book for a social behavior study, so be it. I can only give the words that my life experiences have been. So that means, God (Jesus) is mentioned throughout the book.

People have tried so many vices to bring happiness into their lives and have still come up disappointed. The completeness or wholeness they search for will never be found with material pos-

sessions or in relationships with other humans. It is beyond our understanding as to how something spiritual can make us feel good, can take us into a secret place and hold us as if we are babies. The spiritual can calm our fears and go before us, making ways out of no ways. Yes, Jesus performs miracles. Why do I say 'miracles'? When something takes place that humans have neither understanding of or control of, it's a miracle. How can we explain them? We can't.

Jada makes note that the sorrow that surrounded her when she entered the room has been lifted. Smiling, she says,

I feel my tears drying. For the first time I know if I please God, I am free from my fears. Fear of failure can no longer stand between me and what God would have me say. In spite of what I might think the cost to me is, I must tell others what God has done for me and will do for any person who seeks to be an over comer. Regardless of our past sins, God really does heal us as we go forward in His name! We must, in turn, speak even if there is only one person to hear about Jesus. Be they on skid row or in the White House, we must speak. Out of our bellies flow rivers of living water. God has predestined us for this purpose.

Chapter 5

AS I WENT, I WAS HEALED

Regardless of our past, God uses
our being broken as a light to show
others the way to Him. As we travel
toward God, we are healed.

The only reason for reviewing your past is to learn so that you will understand how the past has prepared you to fulfill your future purpose. Jada shares her journey that results in her continuous and gradual healing. She points out,

> *I realize that many of my desires were not sinful, but I lacked the right timing or the right person. I would justify my actions. In the final analysis, I was deceiving myself.*
>
> *I did not come into a sense of sexual fulfillment until I was older. I had to get beyond my sense of condemnation. This was not possible until I sought the place where the seeds of condemnation were originally planted during my earlier years. Positive role models were needed for me to achieve this wholeness. Once, I studied the Bible for myself, I found that many things I had been told and taught were not biblical facts. I discovered*

that sexuality is a gift from God, and a man and woman are intended to come together to share this gift. I finally realize the battle is in my mind and I have control over my body. There is nothing physically wrong with me. The more time I spend with God, the greater is my healing.

The question is what do I have to say that has not already been said? The answer is: To whom much is given, much is required. Luke 12:48 (NIV). In God's healing me, delivering me, and restoring me, Jesus has given me a purpose! I am a vessel to be used to direct others to God.

Jada is excited as she talks about her God-given purpose. She says God has given everyone a gift, and she believes her gift is Mercy. She explains,

My relationship with God is a love relationship I have never had before. It is a great gift because there is no condemnation. I feel safe in opening my heart   to God. For the first time in my life, I know unconditional love and know God will never leave me. God intends for me to love others just as He has given this love to me.

Jada remembers questioning God about this gift of mercy. Too often mercy is not a good and comfortable feeling.

Monica Young-Freeman

I can look at someone without knowing them and see their pain through smiles or attire, that implies status, title or material wealth.

Jada has come to believe this gift is what God gave her as part of her ministry to others.

Needless to say, I have also begun to have mercy for those who have hurt me. I want to understand what has happened to make them as they are. My love for God has grown stronger as I have begun to see my prayers being answered for others.

Jada thinks back to when she was in her mid twenties, and she discovers there is more to God than anything she had experienced.

I couldn't explain the feeling, but I knew it was the Holy Spirit pricking at my heart and giving me the desire to want more.

She also remembers having the desire to travel overseas to do missionary work.

The question of how I would support myself if I quit my job stood in the way. It was years later when I visited Kenya (Africa) and saw the poverty, hunger, sickness and homelessness, that I knew this was indeed part of God's plan for me. I wanted to understand this motivational gift.

Jada describes herself as becoming more sensitive to the hurts of others rather than to their joys. She has been drawn to people in distress. Praying for the mental distress of others has evolved into being her particular interest. Words and actions and the resulting hurt prick at her heart. She finds a sense of unity with those who are sensitive to the needs and feelings of others. She finds she is spiritually closed to those who are insincere or insensitive. Jada talks about "self mercy."

This is the mercy that takes the focus off God's Holy Spirit and strengthens one's ability to empathize. In this mercy, there is also evidence of resentment toward others who are not sensitive to personal needs, who fail to be firm when necessary. Those who excuse or make allowances for the behavior of others, thus appearing weak and indecisive, and those who are insincere or insensitive fall into this category. I don't want to appear this way, because there are those who feel my sensitivity to the Holy Spirit and my sensitivity to the feelings of others may cause me to be guided by emotions, rather than by logic.

Monica Young-Freeman

She expresses concern about the members of the opposite sex who might misinterpret her actions as weak because they can't discern her spiritual gift. This concern is also felt when she interacts with those who might think the words and actions, of others, causing emotional hurt and pain, are not her business. She also finds her ability to discern insincerity, on occasion, causes others to have difficulty getting to know her. Her spiritual sensitivity causes some others to be reluctant to be frank in her presence for fear of offending or hurting her. She sits and reflects, for awhile, her fate and the happenings in her past in which this gift of spiritual sensitivity may have saved her life. She thinks of the miracle that occurred after a life-threatening event in her life.

It has been over eight years, but I still recall the day as if it were today. It is a hot summer morning. I am driving down Lake Shore Drive on my way to work. A feeling of fear makes me more aware of the ordinary things around me. I don't know which moment will be my last. This particular beautiful morning, I pay attention to the birds and the jewel-colored lake that stretches along beside me as I drive.

I have made the decision to no longer hide from the man who is now my ex-husband for the second time. I exit Lake Shore Drive and enter the parking garage near my work. I pull into a stall, open the car door and glance into my rear view mirror. I see something make a quick movement. It is my ex-husband. He instructs me to get back into my car. Instead, I decide I am not going to let him get into my car. I get out of the car and he stands beside me. I begin to try to make my way between parked cars onto the ramp. My hope is to draw some attention and to escape. My ex-husband follows, looking deranged. He doesn't seem to be the man I had known. I can't find the words to describe him. He tells me he wants me to go with him and watch him kill himself. I tell him, 'I am not going with you.' My voice is loud so as to attract others. 'You don't have to do this lets pray!' He answers, 'It's too late there is nothing that God can do for me now.

Once I see the gun, I become more frightened. I decide I don't want to stay in a deserted area where no one can find me. My heart is pounding so hard it feels as if it is coming out of my chest. My thoughts begin to flash to God. Am I going to die at thirty-nine? My thoughts are interrupted as he tells me to come with him or he will shoot me.

I try to persuade him to pray with me. He keeps repeating, 'If you don't come with me, you are going to die.' A security guard approaches us and my ex-husband tells me if I say anything, he will kill the guard and me. When the security man comes closer, he notices my fear and my ex-husband's extreme agitation. The guard tells my ex-husband to leave the garage or he will call the police. My ex-husband tells the guard, 'She is my wife and I am not leaving.' The security guard leaves to call for help. I've been told the shooting begins when the flashing police cars arrive. I only remember responding to the gun fire by raising both of my hands. I feel excruciating pain in my wrist. I don't remember the bullets that enter my jaw and ear. As I fall to my knees, I am choking on my blood. I look up at my ex-husband and he is looking at me. He takes his foot and pushes me over. My first thought is to close my eyes and pretend to be dead. He shoots again. I am in and out of consciousness, but I am aware of blood dripping on me. I don't know if it is blood from his self-inflicted wound or if it is my blood.

The next thing I am aware of is the inside of the hospital emergency room. I have been shot five times. There is unbearable pain that seems to be caused by a procedure being done without anesthetics. I am told later that a tube is being inserted because my lungs are filling with blood.

91

Because I am fighting to survive, they do sedate me. I hear them say, 'you are at the hospital.'

During one conscious moment, I ask my sister where my ex-husband is. 'You don't have to worry about him any more,' is her response. But this is not enough to reassure me. I am still driven by fear and want to know he can no longer hurt me. She doesn't tell me, at that time, that he is dead. She doesn't think I am ready to handle that information, yet. Although, the physical pain is great, I have not thought about death. I later find out that the doctors originally give a negative prognosis, thinking I might not make it. If I do survive, they are uncertain about the final outcome and my complete recovery.

I am transferred to another hospital for an available life-saving procedure because a bullet has severed a main blood vessel leading to my brain. I have no idea as to how I look. One of the paramedics decides to take me through a rear entrance so as to attract less attention. I am later told that my head is twice its normal size. The saints (members of my church) gather and pray. The doctors say normally no one is permitted in the recovery room. The doctors are so pleased I make it through the procedure, an exception is made. So the saints receive special permission, thanks to my sister.

God has miraculously brought me through physically and mentally. I realize that if God had only healed my body, but not my mind, I may not have been able to realize his miraculous power. I could not share with others the event that had changed my life.

My pastor's prayers and words, 'God will never leave you. God is with you in whatever you have to face.' There is such assurance in those promises, I know he has aided greatly in my recovery.

My hospital stay lasts for thirteen days. Six days are spent in intensive care and seven days in a regular hospital room. Loved ones devise a way for me to communicate, in spite of my condition. My sister writes the alphabet on a sheet of paper and I point to the letters to make words. My aunt, on my father's side, brings a laptop computer so I can type out words. My immediate family is nearby offering loving support every day.

My first night in a regular room, no longer with the team of health care professionals and surrounding friends and family, I feel alone and helpless. My jaw is wired, and I have chest tubes on both sides of my body. My body is sore from the impact of the bullets and from being confined in the bed. I am unable to move or to call out. Satan comes to visit. I hear Satan say, 'Look at you! You can't do for yourself. How are you going to deal with knowing another person killed himself because of you? Who is going to assist you? You don't even know the outcome of your condition.' It is such a long night. I cry because of this demonic attack on my mind and its spiritual torment.

The spiritual armor to withstand the attack of Satan includes a VCR from one of my prayer partners. She brings gospel video tapes for me to watch, also, a tape player. They allow me to view and listen to gospel songs such as 'Show Up, Healing in His Wings' around the clock. This one song is my saving grace. It provides a shield for my mind. It brings to life the Scripture Isaiah 26:3 (AMP), *God will keep thee in perfect peace whose mind is stayed on Him.*

God places ordinary people in strategic places to carry out His work. The church I attend has members from all walks of life. Jada thinks back over the list of those who respond and says,

It was for no other reason than I am a child of God *that He decided to outpour a miracle in my life. The person who hears the call that came into the Chicago Fire Department paramedic unit is one of my church deacons. When he hears the call, he calls an evangelist who in turn calls my pastor. I was told one of the reporters covering the story is a church member. I think about how God allows things to happen. I could have been shot at home or in my car and left to die. The story is picked up nationally and I receive cards, letters, prayers and financial gifts from near and far. So many of the people coming to the hospital to visit identify themselves as my sisters or other relatives. A nurse asks me, 'How many relatives do you have?' Every time the doctors have doubt in their voices about my recovery, the saints respond, 'Not so!' They anoint me with oil and keep an around-the-clock prayer vigil.*

Once when being lured back into the arms of shame and ejection, I say to my godmother, 'No man is going to look at me again.' She reminds me, in spite of the paralysis in my face, 'God had not brought you this far to leave you now. He said he would restore everything.'

Loosed

My hospital insurance doesn't cover the cost of a private nurse, but God puts people in place to take care of me. A prayer warrior from my old church, who I had not talked with for years, comes to be my private duty nurse. No charge! This is a humbling time for one who thought love comes through the body. I look like a dried-up prune and, yet, my cup is filled to the brim and running over. Friends sleep on cots at the hospital so that I will not be alone. They take me to the bathroom and wipe me, bathe my body, feed me, comb my hair, and clean my nails of the dried accumulation of blood. A prayer warrior gives up her prayer room in her home so that I can continue to recover in an environment including prayer and music. My family understands this is significant to a speedy recovery.

The money offered for these services is refused. Finally, this is the unconditional love I have so sought. Once again, I am reminded of the importance of being careful for what we pray. It was love healing me. Love giving me courage and hope. Through God's love, the kindness of ordinary people show me unconditional love. God meets us where we are and enables us to go where ever He destines.

I have shared my testimony with many people who desire to understand, not only the physical aspects of my healing, but the equally important spiritual and psychological healing. My original fear is that people wonder why I allowed myself to remain a victim. My fear that they might spend their time trying to analyze my mind, asking 'What makes her tick?' has not happened. Instead, they say they admire my strength and can see God played the all-important role in my miraculous recovery.

I believed at the time I was shot that all was well with my soul. I had no question about where I was going to go. I was going to be with Jesus. At the time of the shooting, I did not pray. God allows the media to be there, and, in addition to it being a newsworthy story, prayer warriors, throughout the country, receive an alert that one of the warriors is down. In my imagination, I see Jesus going to God, saying, 'They are getting on my nerves. They are bombarding heaven about her. They act as if she is the only person needing prayer right now. So, God, what shall I do?' I imagine God saying, 'Release her. Let her stay a little while longer.'

I believe this is miraculous. Many others have been through what I have gone through and didn't make it. It has nothing to do with my being a better or deeper person. It is God's plan and, perhaps, one of the hundreds of people who prayed has a direct connection with Jesus. I don't know whose prayer it was or how it came about. What I do know is God performed one of His miracles on me. The moral of my story is that I am one of the ordinary people God has chosen to use to show others His Divine Love. He has chosen to show, even out of the hands of death, He can snatch us and restore us to a state exceeding where we were when the trouble began. It is through His grace and not my merit that this healing miracle was performed. I am compelled to tell any person who wants to hear what God will do for any of us because of His everlasting love for us. Psychiatrists, psychologists, and surgeons can heal others but all heal through the final grace of the Almighty and Everlasting God.

*   *   *   *   *

Monica Young-Freeman

**The following Scriptures were significant in helping me
to overcome challenging events in my life.**

June 20, 1995: The period prior to my being shot.
****

Psalm 118:17

> I will not die, but live,
> And tell of the works of the LORD.

Isaiah 41:13

> For I am the LORD your God, who upholds your right hand,
> Who says to you, 'Do not fear, I will help you.'

Psalm 46:10

> Cease striving and know that I am God;
> I will be exalted among the nations,
> I will be exalted in the earth.

Psalm 62:1-2

> God Alone a Refuge from Treachery and Oppression.
> My soul waits in silence for God only;
> From Him is my salvation.
> He only is my rock and my salvation,
> My stronghold; I shall not be greatly shaken.

Loosed

2 Chronicles 20:17

'You need not fight in this battle; station
yourselves, stand and see the salvation of
the LORD on your behalf, O Judah and Jerusalem.
Do not fear or be dismayed; tomorrow go out to
face them, for the LORD is with you.'

Revelation 12:11

And they overcame him because of the blood of the
Lamb and because of the word of their testimony,
and they did not love their life even when faced
with death.

Romans 9:20-22

On the contrary, who are you, O man, who answers
back to God? The thing molded will not say to the
molder, 'Why did you make me like this, will it?

Or does not the potter have a right over the clay, to
make from the same lump one vessel for honorable use and
another for common use?

What if God, although willing to demonstrate His
wrath and to make His power known, endured with much
patience vessels of wrath prepared for destruction?

Monica Young-Freeman

Proverbs 19:21

>Many plans are in a man's heart,
>But the counsel of the LORD will stand.

Proverbs 20:22

>Do not say, 'I will repay evil';
>Wait for the LORD, and He will save you.

Psalm 27:1-6

>The LORD is my light and my salvation;
>Whom shall I fear?
>The LORD is the defense of my life;
>Whom shall I dread?
>
>When evildoers came upon me to devour my flesh,
>My adversaries and my enemies, they stumbled and fell.
>
>Though a host encamp against me,
>My heart will not fear;
>Though war arise against me,
>In spite of this I shall be confident.
>
>One thing I have asked from the LORD, that I shall seek:
>That I may dwell in the house of the LORD all the days of my life,
>To behold the beauty of the LORD

Loosed

And to meditate in His temple.
For in the day of trouble He will conceal me in His tabernacle;
In the secret place of His tent He will hide me;
He will lift me up on a rock.

And now my head will be lifted up above my enemies
around me, And I will offer in His tent sacrifices with shouts of
joy; I will sing, yes, I will sing praises to the LORD.

Isaiah 48:22

'There is no peace for the wicked,' says the LORD.

Romans 3:17

And the path of peace they have not known.

Jeremiah 33:3

'Call to Me and I will answer you,
and I will tell you great and mighty things,
which you do not know.'

2 Thessalonians 3:3

But the Lord is faithful, and He will strengthen
and protect you from the evil one

Galatians 5:22

But the fruit of the Spirit is love, joy, peace,
patience, kindness, goodness, faithfulness.

Isaiah 26:3

The steadfast of mind You will keep in perfect peace,
Because he trusts in You.

Psalm 55:22

Cast your burden upon the LORD and He will sustain you;
He will never allow the righteous to be shaken.

Isaiah: 41:10

'Do not fear, for I am with you;
Do not anxiously look about you, for I am your God.
I will strengthen you, surely I will help you,
Surely I will uphold you with My righteous right hand.'

Habakkuk 2:1

I will stand on my guard post
And station myself on the rampart;
And I will keep watch to see what He will speak to me,
And how I may reply when I am reproved

Loosed

Deuteronomy 20:1-4

When you go out to battle against your enemies and see horses and chariots and people more numerous than you, do not be afraid of them; for the LORD your God, who brought you up from the land of Egypt, is with you.

When you are approaching the battle, the priest shall come near and speak to the people.

He shall say to them, 'Hear, O Israel, you are approaching the battle against your enemies today. Do not be fainthearted. Do not be afraid, or panic, or tremble before them, for the LORD your God is the one who goes with you, to fight for you against your enemies, to save you.'

Psalm 23:1

The LORD is my shepherd,
I shall not want.

Deuteronomy 20:7

'And who is the man that is engaged to a woman and has not married her? Let him depart and return to his house, otherwise he might die in the battle and another man would marry her.'

Deuteronomy 3:22

'Do not fear them, for the LORD your God is the one
fighting for you.'

Deuteronomy 31:8

'The LORD is the one who goes ahead of you;
He will be with you. He will not fail you or forsake
you. Do not fear or be dismayed.'

1 John 5

For whatever is born of God overcomes the world;
and this is the victory that has overcome the world
our faith.

Isaiah 55

So will My word be which goes forth from My mouth;
It will not return to Me empty,
Without accomplishing what I desire,
And without succeeding in the matter for which I sent it.

Loosed

Matthew 18:19-20

'Again I say to you, that if two of you agree on earth about anything that they may ask, it shall be done for them by My Father who is in heaven.

'For where two or three have gathered together in My name, I am there in their midst.'

Proverbs 10:25

When the whirlwind passes, the wicked is no more,
But the righteous has an everlasting foundation.

Proverbs 10:27

The fear of the LORD prolongs life,
But the years of the wicked will be shortened.

2 Corinthians 4:16-18

Therefore we do not lose heart, but though our outer man is decaying, yet our inner man is being renewed day by day.
For momentary, light affliction is producing for us an eternal weight of glory far beyond all comparison,
While we look not at the things which are seen, but at the things which are not seen; for the things which are seen are temporal, but the things which are not seen are eternal.

Monica Young-Freeman

Psalm 22:8

'Commit yourself to the LORD; let Him deliver him;
Let Him rescue him, because He delights in him.'

Romans 16:20

The God of peace will soon crush Satan under your feet.
The grace of our Lord Jesus be with you.

Romans 12:19

Never take your own revenge, beloved, but leave room
for the   wrath of God, for it is written, 'VENGEANCE IS MINE,
I WILL REPAY,' says the Lord.

Exodus 23:22

'But if you truly obey his voice and do all that I say, then
I will be an enemy to your enemies and an adversary to your
adversaries.'

Psalm 32:8

I will instruct you and teach you in the way which you
should go; I will counsel you with My eye upon you.

Loosed

Psalm 126:5

Those who sow in tears shall reap with joyful shouting.

Proverbs 4:4

Then he taught me and said to me,
'Let your heart hold fast my words;
Keep my commandments and live;'

Psalm 37:1-40

A Psalm of David.

Do not fret because of evildoers,
Be not envious toward wrongdoers.
For they will wither quickly like the grass
And fade like the green herb.

Trust in the LORD and do good;
Dwell in the land and ultimate faithfulness.

Delight yourself in the LORD;
And He will give you the desires of your heart.

Commit your way to the LORD,
Trust also in Him, and He will do it.

Monica Young-Freeman

He will bring forth your righteousness as the light
And your judgment as the noonday.

Rest in the LORD and wait patiently for Him;
Do not fret because of him who prospers in his way,
Because of the man who carries out wicked schemes.

Cease from anger and forsake wrath;
Do not fret; it leads only to evildoing.

For evildoers will be cut off,
But those who wait for the LORD, they will inherit the land.

Yet a little while and the wicked man will be no more;
And you will look carefully for his place and he will not
be there.
But the humble will inherit the land
And will delight themselves in abundant prosperity.

The wicked plots against the righteous
And gnashes at him with his teeth.

The Lord laughs at him,
For He sees his day is coming.

The wicked have drawn the sword and bent their bow
To cast down the afflicted and the needy,

Loosed

To slay those who are upright in conduct.

Their sword will enter their own heart,
And their bows will be broken.

Better is the little of the righteous
Than the abundance of many wicked.

For the arms of the wicked will be broken,
But the LORD sustains the righteous.
The LORD knows the days of the blameless,
And their inheritance will be forever.

They will not be ashamed in the time of evil,
And in the days of famine they will have abundance.
But the wicked will perish;
And the enemies of the LORD will be like the glory of
the pastures,
They vanish like smoke they vanish away.

The wicked borrows and does not pay back,
But the righteous is gracious and gives.

For those blessed by Him will inherit the land,
But those cursed by Him will be cut off.

The steps of a man are established by the LORD,

Monica Young-Freeman

And He delights in his way.

When he falls, he will not be hurled headlong,
Because the LORD is the One who holds his hand.

I have been young and now I am old,
Yet I have not seen the righteous forsaken
Or his descendants begging bread.

All day long he is gracious and lends,
And his descendants are a blessing.

Depart from evil and do good,
So you will abide forever.

For the LORD loves justice
And does not forsake His godly ones;
They are preserved forever,
But the descendants of the wicked will be cut off.

The righteous will inherit the land
And dwell in it forever.

The mouth of the righteous utters wisdom,
And his tongue speaks justice.

The law of his God is in his heart;

Loosed

His steps do not slip.

The wicked spies upon the righteous
And seeks to kill him.

The LORD will not leave him in his hand
Or let him be condemned when he is judged.

Wait for the LORD and keep His way,
And He will exalt you to inherit the land;
When the wicked are cut off, you will see it.

I have seen a wicked, violent man
spreading himself like a luxuriant tree in its native soil.

Then he passed away, and lo, he was no more;
I sought for him, but he could not be found.
Mark the blameless man, and behold the upright;
For the man of peace will have a posterity.

But transgressors will be altogether destroyed;
The posterity of the wicked will be cut off.

But the salvation of the righteous is from the LORD;
He is their strength in time of trouble.

The LORD helps them and delivers them;

He delivers them from the wicked and saves them,
Because they take refuge in Him.

****
**The next set of Scriptures sustained me after I came out
of the wilderness-6/23/95.**
****

Psalm 30:5

For His anger is but for a moment,
His favor is for a lifetime;
Weeping may last for the night,
But a shout of joy comes in the morning.

Psalm 23:1-6

The LORD is my shepherd,
[1]Shall not want.

[2]He makes me lie down in green pastures;
He leads me beside quiet waters.

[3]He restores my soul;
He guides me in the paths of righteousness
For His name's sake.

Loosed

⁴Even though I walk through the valley of the shadow of death,
I fear no evil, for You are with me;
Your rod and Your staff, they comfort me.

⁵You prepare a table before me in the presence of my enemies;
You have anointed my head with oil; My cup overflows.
⁶Surely goodness and loving kindness will follow me
all the days of my life,
And I will dwell in the house of the LORD forever.

John 6:33

'For the bread of God is that which comes down out
of heaven, and gives life to the world.'

John 5:24

'Truly, truly, I say to you, he who hears My word, and
believes Him who sent Me, has eternal life, and does not come
into judgment, but has passed out of death into life.

John 11:25

Jesus said to her, " I am the resurrection and the life;
he who believes in Me will live even if he dies,

Monica Young-Freeman

Romans 6:4-5

Therefore we have been buried with Him through baptism into death, so that as Christ was raised from the dead through the glory of the Father, so we too might walk in newness of life.

For if we have become united with Him in the likeness of His death, certainly we shall also be in the likeness of His resurrection,

Romans 8:11

But if the Spirit of Him who raised Jesus from the dead dwells in you, He who raised Christ Jesus from the dead will also give life to your mortal bodies through His Spirit who dwells in you.

Colossians 3:1-17

Therefore if you have been raised up with Christ, keep seeking the things above, where Christ is, seated at the right hand of God.

Set your mind on the things above, not on the things that are on earth.

Loosed

For you have died and your life is hidden with Christ in God.

When Christ, who is our life, is revealed, then you also will be revealed with Him in glory.

Therefore consider the members of your earthly body as dead to immorality, impurity, passion, evil desire, and greed, which amounts to idolatry.

For it is because of these things that the wrath of God will come upon the sons of disobedience, and in them you also once walked, when you were living in them.

But now you also, put them all aside: anger, wrath, malice, slander, and abusive speech from your mouth.

Do not lie to one another, since you laid aside the old self with its evil practices, and have put on the new self who is being renewed to a true knowledge according to the image of the One who created him a renewal in which there is no distinction between Greek and Jew, circumcised and uncircumcised, bar barian, Scythian, slave and freeman, but Christ is all, and in all.

So, as those who have been chosen of God, holy and beloved, put on a heart of compassion, kindness, humility gentleness and patience; bearing with one another, and forgiving each other, whoever has a complaint against anyone; just as the Lord forgave you, so also should you.

Beyond all these things put on love, which is the perfect bond of unity.

Let the peace of Christ rule in your hearts, to which indeed you were called in one body; and be thankful.

Let the word of Christ richly dwell within you, with all wisdom teaching and admonishing one another with psalms and hymns and spiritual songs, singing with thankfulness in your hearts to God.

Whatever you do in word or deed, do all in the name of the Lord Jesus, giving thanks through Him to God the Father.

Galatians 5:16

But I say, walk by the Spirit, and you will not carry out the desire of the flesh.

Romans 12:1

Therefore I urge you, brethren, by the mercies of God, to present your bodies a living and holy sacrifice, acceptable to God, which is your spiritual service of worship.

Colossians 1:9-11 and 13-14

Loosed

^{9}For this reason also, since the day we heard of it, we have not ceased to pray for you and to ask that you may be filled with the knowledge of His will in all spiritual wisdom and understanding,

^{10}So that you will walk in a manner worthy of the Lord, to please Him in all respects, bearing fruit in every good work and increasing in the knowledge of God;

^{11}Strengthened with all power, according to His glorious might, for the attaining of all steadfastness and patience; joyously the inheritance of the saints in Light.

^{13}For He rescued us from the domain of darkness, and transferred us to the kingdom of His beloved Son,

^{14}In whom we have redemption, the forgiveness of sins.

Monica Young-Freeman

Loosed

Monica Young-Freeman

For more information about this author please visit

www.intimepublishing.com

Loosed

The Author

Monica Young-Freeman and husband resides in Chicago, Illinois, where she has been a member of Apostolic Church of God for over 15 years. She has spoken before medical students and faculty at Northwestern University, Dwight Correctional Center, and various churches. Interviewed by Fox News TV - On Domestic Violence in the Workplace, NBC News, documentary of her own experience in between airing of the Movie 'Every Nine Seconds', with regards to women being murdered by there partners. She also has been aired on TV-38 "Amongest Friends," a christian Tv program, interviewed sharing her own testimony of being shot five times by her ex-husband. She desires to share her life experiences in hope that others will be set free and most of all that God's purposes will be fulfilled in all lives !